Discovering Mission
San Gabriel Arcángel

BY MADELINE STEVENS

Cavendish
Square

New York

Published in 2015 by Cavendish Square Publishing, LLC
243 5th Avenue, Suite 136, New York, NY 10016

Copyright © 2015 by Cavendish Square Publishing, LLC

First Edition

Website: cavendishsq.com

This publication represents the opinions and views of the author based on his or her personal experience, knowledge, and research. The information in this book serves as a general guide only. The author and publisher have used their best efforts in preparing this book and disclaim liability rising directly or indirectly from the use and application of this book.

CPSIA Compliance Information: Batch #WS14CSQ

All websites were available and accurate when this book was sent to press.

Library of Congress Cataloging-in-Publication Data

Stevens, Madeline.
Discovering Mission San Gabriel Arcángel / Madeline Stevens.
pages cm. — (California missions)
Includes index.
ISBN 978-1-62713-115-5 (hardcover) ISBN 978-1-62713-117-9 (ebook)
1. Mission San Gabriel Arcangel (San Gabriel, Calif.)—History—Juvenile literature. 2. Spanish mission buildings—California—San Gabriel Region—History—Juvenile literature. 3. Franciscans—California—San Gabriel Region—History—Juvenile literature. 4. Gabrielino Indians—Missions—California—San Gabriel Region—History—Juvenile literature. 5. California—History—To 1846—Juvenile literature. I. Title.

F869.M655M34 2015
979.4'93—dc23

2014005325

Editorial Director: Dean Miller
Editor: Kristen Susienka
Copy Editor: Cynthia Roby
Art Director: Jeffrey Talbot
Designer: Douglas Brooks
Photo Researcher: J8 Media
Production Manager: Jennifer Ryder-Talbot
Production Editor: David McNamara

Printed in the United States of America

CALIFORNIA
MISSIONS

Contents

Mission San Gabriel was one of the most successful of the Alta California missions.

1
The Spanish Expand Their Empire

Tucked away in downtown San Gabriel stands a large fortress-style church building that looks somewhat out of place in modern California. Yet the structure played a primary role, both good and bad, in the history of the region. Named for Saint Gabriel, Holy Prince of Archangels, Mission San Gabriel Arcángel's story tells of struggle, accomplishment, difficulties, and the founding of one of the great cities in North America.

STAKING A CLAIM

The Spanish first arrived along the coast of what they called *Alta*, or "upper," California in 1542. Explorer Juan Rodríguez Cabrillo sailed out of Navidad, near Manzanillo, Mexico, on June 24, to search for legendary wealthy cities and a water route from the North Pacific to the North Atlantic. Neither existed. Cabrillo discovered the Bay of San Diego on September 28. He stopped along the shores of Santa Catalina and San Pedro on October 6, and the Tongva, the region's indigenous people, canoed out to meet him. They invited him to land but he declined. Members of his

In the 1760s, King Carlos III sent friars and soldiers to Alta California to start missions.

expedition later reached as far north as today's Oregon before returning to Navidad on April 14, 1543.

By the 1760s, King Carlos III of Spain wanted to ensure his claim on this land before Russian or English people settled there. In 1768, the king told the **viceroy**—a person chosen to rule for the king in a new land—of New Spain (today's Mexico) to start settling the northern frontier of New Spain, using the mission system. The king sent his officer, Inspector General José de Gálvez, to help. Spain had already used the mission system to take over land in New Spain, Florida, Texas, and *Baja*, or "lower," California.

In the spring of 1769, the governor of Baja California, an army captain named Gaspár de Portolá, led a group of soldiers, missionaries, and some Christian Native Americans from the Baja California missions into Alta California. Some traveled in three ships. Others, including the president of the missions, Fray Junípero Serra, traveled the 715 miles by land. Their destination was the San Diego harbor, discovered more than 225 years earlier by Cabrillo. Nearly half of the 219-member expedition died or deserted before reaching their destination in early July. One of the three ships was lost at sea.

On July 16, 1769, Fray Serra founded the first of the twenty-one missions near the harbor. He named it San Diego de Alcalá.

2
The
Tongva

The Native Californians near Mission San Gabriel Arcángel belonged to the Tongva tribe. There were many villages—as many as thirty-one known sites spread over a wide area. There were an estimated 5,000 Tongva in the region when the Spanish arrived. Each village was ruled by a group of elders. The Tongva leaders could be men or women, and were called "wots." Each Tongva village also had a religious leader and healer called a **shaman**.

OCEAN TRAVELER

The Tongva and the Chumash, their neighbors to the north and west, were among the few indigenous populations that navigated the ocean. They made plank canoes called *ti'ats* or *tomols*, which were up to 30 feet long. The tomols were large enough to hold twelve men and their goods, and strong enough for ocean travel. These canoes were made from planks held

Like the Tongva, the Chumash used seashells to make jewelry.

together with hemp or dowels. They were then coated with pine pitch and tar, which could be found at the La Brea Tar Pits, or asphaltum that washed ashore from natural oil seeps.

These canoes helped the Tongva and the Chumash to trade with their neighbors, including groups living on Santa Catalina and other Channel Islands.

The Tongva, which means "people of the earth," knew how to survive by living off the land. Their ancestors had lived in the Los Angeles basin for as many as 10,000 years. The women gathered berries, mushrooms, seeds, oats, pine nuts, seaweed, and acorns to eat. They ground the acorns into a mush and cooked it. The men

The Chumash created boats that they used to fish and travel on the waters.

hunted birds and small animals using bows and arrows, sticks, and traps. They caught fish in the rivers and in the sea and believed they were the "Lords of the Ocean."

They were also skilled at making baskets of different shapes and sizes, wood carvings, boxes, and tools from stone. Their skills brought them great benefits. In fact, anthropologist Lowell John Bean described the Tongva who occupied most of present-day Los Angeles County as "the wealthiest, most populous, and most powerful" group in Southern California after the Chumash.

The Tongva, like many of the tribes native to California, were thankful to the land for giving them what they needed to live.

They believed that they had been created from the land. They gave many thanks to their creator. They did not believe in evil spirits or any concept of hell. They considered owls and porpoises sacred and never hunted them.

The indigenous people bathed daily in nearby waterways. They carved bowls, pipes, and beads from a soft rock called steatite (soapstone). In the winter, they kept warm with blankets and capes they had made from feathers, rabbit fur, or sea otter skins.

SHOW OF COURAGE

Courage was considered a highly honorable trait and failure to show it brought on disgrace. Men would lie on red anthills to prove their courage. Boys faced trials by fire, whipping, and lying on anthills to test their courage. If they failed these trials they were considered weak and cowardly. Yet despite the importance they placed on courage, the Tongva did not go to war often, and murder and robbery were rare.

One of the skills nearly lost by the tribes of the region was canoe building. The last canoes for fishing built by the Chumash were constructed in 1850. In 1913, a 110-year-old Chumash man named Fernando Librado constructed a tomol, which he had seen made in his youth, for an anthropologist, John Harrington, who took notes. In recent decades several canoes have been made with the use of those notes.

The Tongva became known as the Gabrieliños after the arrival of the Spanish.

3
The
Mission System

There were twenty-one missions established in Alta California and all were built using the labor of the Native Americans. The mission system had two goals: to provide citizens for Spain so it could hold its claim on Alta California, and to allow the **Franciscan** friars, such as Fray Junípero Serra, to spread their religion. The Native Americans knew nothing of this plan.

NEED FOR CITIZENS

Spanish missions were small communities governed by friars. The plan was that the missions would later be turned into *pueblos*, or Spanish towns, and the indigenous people would become Spanish citizens and live there.

The friars believed that **Catholicism** was the one true religion. They wanted to "save" people who were not Christian by converting them to Catholicism. The missionaries believed Catholicism would save the Native Americans' souls.

Presidios, or forts for soldiers, would be built to provide protection for the missions. The indigenous people would be taught to farm to meet the needs of the mission and would provide food and drink for the soldiers. At older missions, the

Spaniards discovered that if the neophytes—Native Americans who were newly baptized into the Catholic faith—could leave the missions, many would not return. They would forget what they had learned, lose their clothing, and return to their old ways. Yet the friars believed the missions taught the Native people a better, more civilized, way of life.

CHANGE NOT ALLOWED

The choice to convert to Catholicism was voluntary, but the Franciscans didn't allow anyone to change their mind. Fray Pedro Font, who visited Mission San Gabriel Arcángel in 1776,

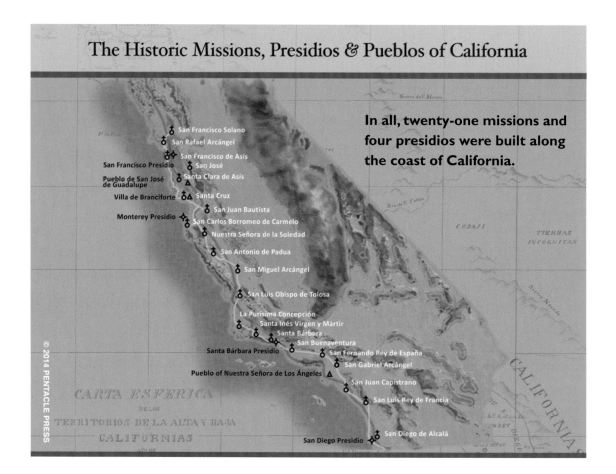

The Historic Missions, Presidios & Pueblos of California

In all, twenty-one missions and four presidios were built along the coast of California.

San Francisco Solano
San Rafael Arcángel
San Francisco de Asís
San Francisco Presidio
San José
Pueblo de San José de Guadalupe
Santa Clara de Asís
Villa de Branciforte
Santa Cruz
San Juan Bautista
Monterey Presidio
San Carlos Borromeo de Carmelo
Nuestra Señora de la Soledad
San Antonio de Padua
San Miguel Arcángel
San Luis Obispo de Tolosa
La Purísima Concepción
Santa Inés Virgen y Mártir
Santa Bárbara
Santa Bárbara Presidio
San Buenaventura
San Fernando Rey de España
Pueblo of Nuestra Señora de Los Ángeles
San Gabriel Arcángel
San Juan Capistrano
San Luis Rey de Francia
San Diego de Alcalá
San Diego Presidio

© 2014 PENTACLE PRESS

CARTA ESFERICA DE LOS TERRITORIOS DE LA ALTA Y BAJA CALIFORNIAS

CALIFORNIA

The people who joined the mission system had to live by strict rules.

wrote: "Since the Indians are accustomed to living in the fields and the hills like beasts, the fathers require that if they wish to be Christians they shall no longer go to the forest, but must live in the mission; and if they leave … they will go to seek them and punish them."

The friars needed the Tongva and other tribesmen to construct buildings, plant crops, and live at the missions. The friars offered gifts to the Native people to lure them to join the missions, and the Native people did not understand the reason behind the friendly behavior. They were unaware that they would be tricked into giving up their land, their religion, and their old way of life, and forced into slave-like working conditions.

4
Mission San Gabriel Arcángel Begins

Gaspár de Portolá left San Diego shortly after his arrival because he had orders to settle another port, farther north, which the Spanish called Monterey, after their viceroy. Portolá's party traveled on foot up the coast to find Monterey. When they encountered dangerous sea cliffs, they traveled inland through canyons.

At one point, the group camped by a river. There were several earthquakes while they stayed there, so they named the river *Río San Gabriel de Los Temblores*. *Temblores* means "earthquakes" in Spanish. Near this river, Fray Juan Crespí, a friar in Portolá's party, wrote in his diary: "We came to a valley with a beautiful river. There is a large plain and good land for planting. It is the best place we have seen for a mission."

LEGEND OF A LADY

Fray Serra appointed Fray Ángel Fernandez de Somera and Fray Pedro Benito Cambón to be its founding fathers. There is a legend, however, about the founding of Mission San Gabriel Arcángel. As the story goes, when the Spaniards neared the river described by Fray Crespí, members of the Tongva who were angry about the Spanish presence came armed with bows and arrows. One of the friars unrolled a painting of Our Lady of Sorrows—one of the names by which Catholics refer to the Virgin Mary. He showed it to the Tongva, who then dropped their weapons. The chiefs placed their necklaces on the ground at the feet of the "Beautiful Queen." The others followed.

Frays Cambón and Somera considered that particular spot of land unsuitable and continued searching until coming to a hill

At Mission San Gabriel, neophytes built the buildings and decorated the inside with works of art, such as this depiction of the second Station of the Cross.

near a stream in the San Miguel Valley. On it, the friars raised a large cross, and on September 8, 1771, the fourth mission was founded. It was called Mission San Gabriel Arcángel, named for Saint Gabriel, God's messenger angel.

The Native Americans, still fascinated by the missionaries, were willing helpers. They assisted the friars in building a shelter of branches over an altar. The friars blessed water from the river and sprinkled it over the cross. They sang Mass, gave a sermon, and rang the new mission bells. The soldiers fired their muskets, and the founding ceremony of San Gabriel Arcángel was complete.

Mission San Gabriel Arcángel was established in September 1771 and became the first California mission depicted in an oil painting (shown above).

BUILDING THE MISSION

The next day, they began to build. They constructed walls from willow poles and roofs from tule—reeds used by the Native people to make homes and boats. They also built a chapel, huts for the friars and the soldiers, and corrals for the animals they had brought. The friars, the soldiers, and the Native people worked hard. Within a few days, the temporary buildings were complete. The soldiers placed sharp poles around the building, in case of attack.

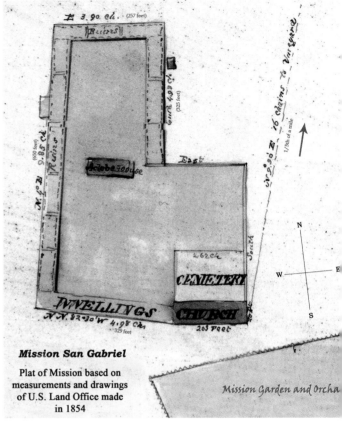

Mission San Gabriel

Plat of Mission based on measurements and drawings of U.S. Land Office made in 1854

This layout of the mission was drawn in 1862 and showed the mission's many buildings.

In 1772, Fray Francisco Palóu and Fray Fermín Lasuén visited and recommended moving to a better site. Four years later, the move was made to avoid spring flooding that ruined crops. Fray Lasuén became president of the missions of Alta California in 1785 after Fray Serra died.

HISTORIC TRAIL

By 1773 there were five missions, two presidios, and about seventy settlers in Alta California. They received supplies once a year by boat. Juan Bautista de Anza, captain of a presidio in Sonora (now southern Arizona), set up a route over land to supply the settlements and then led an expedition with 240 people to settle the port of San Francisco. He left Sonora on October 23, 1775, and arrived at San Gabriel on January 4, 1776. San Gabriel's location on the Juan Bautista de Anza Historic Trail made it an important stop for new settlers.

CONVERTING THE NATIVE PEOPLE

In the first few years, Mission San Gabriel Arcángel's founding fathers visited Native American villages attempting to recruit people for the mission. They told the parents of sick children to have them baptized. If the children died, the act of **baptism** would ensure that their souls would be saved. If the baptized children survived their illness, they became part of the mission. When that happened, the parents usually joined to be with their children.

The friars did many things to convince the Native people to join the mission system. They invited them to visit, showed them religious ornaments, performed rituals, played music, and served Spanish food. Many Native people also visited Mission San Gabriel Arcángel because of Fray Cambón's and Fray Somera's friendliness.

In 1772, Frays Antonio Paterna and Antonio Cruzado took over for Frays Cambón and Somera. Both Frays Cruzado and Paterna served the missions of New Spain for many decades before taking charge of the mission. Cruzado had worked for twenty-two years in Baja California and developed a great knowledge about agriculture. During his thirty-two-year term at Mission San Gabriel Arcángel, Cruzado would design its iconic fortress-style church.

5
Early Days at the Mission

Trouble between the Native Americans, the missionaries, and the soldiers started soon after Mission San Gabriel Arcángel was founded.

TONGVA MISTREATED

Frightened by the presence of so many Tongva, Fray Somera requested more soldiers, many of whom did not respect the Native people, viewing them as uncivilized. One soldier rode his horse into a nearby village and attacked the wife of a Tongva leader. When the leader found out about the attack, he and his tribe went to the mission to kill the soldier. The soldier shot the leader with his musket, then beheaded him and stuck his head on a pole as a warning to other Native Americans. A few days later, the villagers asked for the head so that they could mourn their leader.

For a long time after this incident, the villagers remained far from the mission, and they lost their trust in the soldiers. As a result, growth at the mission slowed. The hardships this caused affected Frays Cambón and Somera, who had become ill. In 1772, Frays Antonio Paterna and Antonio Cruzado stopped at Mission San Gabriel Arcángel on their way to found a new mission. They

Mission San Gabriel Arcángel had many visitors. In its early years, Juan Bautista de Anza traveled with settlers to the mission.

saw the trouble and decided to stay there, allowing Frays Cambón and Somera to retire and leave the mission.

REGAINING TRUST

Frays Paterna and Cruzado worked hard to regain the Native people's trust and keep the soldiers in line. The two frays were gentle and patient. The Native people began offering their children for baptism. Surprisingly, one of the first children to be baptized was the son of the slain Native American leader. He was offered for baptism by his mother.

Mission San Gabriel Arcángel was one of the most successful for the Spanish in Alta California, and it grew steadily under Frays Cruzado and Paterna. Later, Fray Sanchez took over. By 1786 the mission had 1,000 neophytes. At its peak, in 1817, there were 1,701.

The mission herd grew from 128 animals in 1772 to 42,350 at its height in 1829, mostly cattle (25,000) and sheep (15,000). More than 353,000 bushels of wheat, barley, corn, beans, peas, lentils, and garbanzos (chickpeas) were harvested. This was more than any other mission produced. In fact, Mission San Gabriel Arcángel produced such bountiful harvests and large herds of cattle that it became known as "the Queen of the Missions."

In 1790, the friars asked the government to send artisans, or craftsmen, from New Spain to help build the mission buildings. When the stonemasons, blacksmiths, and carpenters arrived at the missions, they helped construct stone fountains, pillars, arches, ironwork, and bell towers.

DIFFERENT DESIGN

Mission San Gabriel Arcángel attracted so many neophytes that it quickly outgrew its church. When Fray Cruzado designed the new church, he was likely thinking of the famous cathedral of Córdoba, Spain, which he had seen as a child. That cathedral was originally a mosque built by the **Moors**. Their buildings influenced many features of Spanish architecture.

The artisans and neophytes of Mission San Gabriel Arcángel constructed the bottom half of the new church with stone and concrete. From the windows up, brick was used. In the Moorish style, they built long, narrow windows. Between each window, they built buttresses, or support columns, with pyramid caps. They also built arched doorways. A flat roof replaced the church's vaulted roof after an earthquake. The finished church looked strong and solid, like a fortress. Its architecture is called "fortress style."

The friars wanted the neophytes to feel good about their church. The neophytes chose rich colors, such as forest green and deep red, to paint and decorate the inside of the church. Colored rocks were crushed and mixed with olive oil to make paint.

In 1805, after fourteen years of work, the church structure was complete. The elderly Frays Cruzado and Paterna died that year. They were both buried within the sanctuary.

San Gabriel's church is considered the best example of fortress-style architecture in a mission church. To the right of the church entrance, a bell tower was built. The **adobe** wall had arched holes in which the mission's bells were hung. The largest bell, called the **angelus** bell, weighed more than 1 ton (0.9 tonne). In 1812, an earthquake toppled the bell tower. It was rebuilt as a *campanario*, or bell wall, at the end of the church's long side wall. Bell ringers climbed an outdoor stone staircase and crossed the loft, where the choir sang, to reach the belfry.

The mission also had a 170-acre vineyard, the largest in all of Alta California. It provided vines for many of the other missions.

In the 1820s, four mills were built to grind flour, make olive oil, and saw wood. Mules powered two of the mills. The other two, a gristmill and sawmill, used waterpower.

This plaque in Sacramento commemorates Mission San Gabriel Arcángel and its bells.

6

A Day at the Mission

The friars who founded each mission were given a thick book of rules. The book included everything Spain had learned from establishing its earlier missions. It told the friars how to convince the Native population to join the mission, the daily schedule to follow, and details such as what color clothing the neophytes should wear.

REGULATED LIFE

Each day at Mission San Gabriel Arcángel, the neophytes woke at sunrise to the ringing of bells. Soon afterward, the angelus bell called them to church. An hour later, another bell announced breakfast, which was *atole*, a hot cereal made of ground, roasted grain.

When the bell rang again, it was time to work. Even children had jobs. The friars and Baja California neophytes taught every neophyte a job. Many men were taught farming. They grew corn, wheat, barley, lentils, garbanzo beans, cotton, onions, garlic, and tomatoes. There were orchards, with orange trees, limes, apples, pears, peaches, pomegranates, figs, and olives. In 1834, San Gabriel reported having 2,333 fruit trees. A 12-foot (3.7-m) cactus hedge was grown to fence in cattle. One year, the hedge bore more than 37,000 bushels of prickly pear fruit. San Gabriel also became famous for producing fine wines.

Neophytes performed different tasks. The men plowed, planted, and built aqueducts to irrigate the fields. Boys guarded the fields from livestock. After harvest, the neophytes threshed the wheat and then ground it into flour. The women and girls made ponchos for the shepherds, habits for the friars, clothing, and blankets, as well as prepared atole for breakfast and dinner, and cooked lunch in kettles over an outside fire.

Lunch was *pozole*, a meat stew with beans, corn, and vegetables, served with tortillas or atole. After lunch was rest time, or *siesta*, from 2 to 4 p.m. Then the bell rang and work resumed.

Many neophyte men worked on *ranchos*, which were farms where the mission's herds were raised. As the mission's gardens and fields took up more room, ranchos were established surrounding the mission. San Gabriel had about fifteen ranchos. Its best-known cattle ranch was called San Bernardino. A *mayordomo*, who was a baptized Native American from New Spain, supervised work on the ranchos. Neophytes herded cattle, milked cows, fed pigs, sheared sheep, groomed horses, and guarded the oxen. They also branded San Gabriel's cattle with a "T" for temblores.

NOTHING WASTED

During *La Matanza*, meaning "the slaughter," cattle were killed and hides were stretched out to dry. The mission wasted nothing. Sheepskin was used for parchment. Meat was eaten and shared with the soldiers at the presidios. Rawhide was used to hang bells and doors. Sometimes the door itself was made from rawhide. Tanned hides were made into saddles, shoes, and the leather jackets worn by soldiers. Sometimes neophytes used hides to trade for other supplies. The fat from cattle was boiled down into tallow, which was used for making soap and candles. Other neophytes prepared sheep's wool for weaving.

Mission San Gabriel Arcángel's workshops were busy. An American trapper named Harrison Rogers stayed at the mission in 1826. He wrote in his diary: "I walked through the workshops. I saw some Indians blacksmithing, some carpentering, others making the woodwork of ploughs, others employed in making spinning wheels for the women to spin on. There is upwards of sixty women employed in spinning yarn and others weaving."

Through the hard work of the neophytes, Mission San Gabriel Arcángel was one of the most successful missions.

The neophytes made wine and olive oil, cheese, and butter. Men learned metalworking, carpentry, farming, masonry, tanning, and herding. Women learned to spin wool, weave, sew, cook, and make candles and soap.

The neophyte children had lessons each morning and afternoon. The friars tried to teach Catholicism in the neophytes' language, but it didn't contain the right words—so the friars taught them Spanish. They taught songs, prayers, and blessings. A group of boys was chosen for a choir. They learned to read, write, sing, and play instruments. During special events, they performed for the mission.

SOME FREE TIME

At 5 p.m. the angelus bell rang for prayers. Supper, at 6 p.m., was atole and, sometimes, mission wine. After dinner there was a little free time. The neophytes could rest, play games, or visit with each other on the mission. At 8 p.m. the bell rang, calling the women back to their quarters for bed. The men went to bed an hour later.

The friars sometimes gave the neophytes breaks from the daily routine. Sabbath was observed on Sunday with morning Mass and lots of free time. The neophytes raced horses, played games, and gambled.

Some of the most important events at a mission were celebrating holy days and festivals. The ringing of mission bells would mix with the sound of firecrackers and music while people danced, feasted, watched bullfights, and played games.

7
The Beginning of the End

Mission San Gabriel Arcángel sat along three important trails. This allowed many soldiers and settlers to stop at the mission during their travels. The friars became tired of visitors because many of them caused trouble and mistreated the Tongva.

UNWELCOME GUESTS

This mistreatment caused many revolts by the Native Americans— the most famous led by Toypurina, a 24-year-old shaman and the daughter of the Gabrieliño chief of the village Jachivit. Along with neophyte Nicolas José, Toypurina co-led a plot against the mission and convinced other village leaders to take part. But a Spanish soldier overheard talk of the plans. On the night of October 25, 1785, the group entered the mission and was defeated without bloodshed. As punishment, Toypurina was exiled from Mission San Gabriel Arcángel after being held there as a prisoner for the duration of her trial. During this time she was also baptized into the Catholic faith, a move that some historians call a survival technique. She was then sent to live out her life farther north, first at Mission San Carlos Borroméo, located near Monterey. In 1799, Toypurina passed away at Mission San Juan Bautista, and was buried there.

Many Native women joined the missions and became neophytes.

The Spanish governor of California, Felipe de Neve, decided to establish a pueblo, or town, near the mission—a place where visitors could stay. In December 1781, the Spanish government founded the new pueblo, naming it *Nuestra Señora de los Angeles del Río de Porciúncula,* meaning "Our Lady of the Angels by the River of Porciúncula." It was constructed 9 miles (14.5 km) from the mission. Later the town shortened its name to Los Angeles.

Los Angeles grew quickly. Within ten years, it boasted twenty-nine adobe houses, a town hall, granaries, barracks, and a guardhouse, all surrounded by an adobe wall. It had a population of 139 people. The settlers of Los Angeles produced more grain than any mission except San Gabriel. The friars allowed some of the mission's best-trained neophytes to work for pay in the fields at the pueblo.

DISPUTE OVER LAND

In the early 1800s, as Los Angeles grew, its settlers became frustrated with Mission San Gabriel Arcángel. The settlers needed land for their herds and farms, but all the nearby land belonged to Missions San Gabriel and San Fernando Rey de España. Because the missions had California's best land, the settlers of California complained.

In 1812, a large earthquake hit the area, leaving the church badly damaged. The bell tower, the friars' rooms, and many workshops were destroyed. It took years of work to repair the damage and build a new campanario. The friars moved into the granary, which they converted to a church in 1813.

The neophytes suffered the most hardship of all. Mission life was not like that in the villages. The neophytes had to wear different clothing, eat different foods, practice a different religion, and perform different types of work. For example, men were used to resting for long periods between hunts. Now they had to follow the mission's strict routine.

In their villages, the indigenous people were free to live with their families. At the mission, unmarried women and neophyte girls over age eleven had to live inside a locked *monjerío*. They slept, ate, and sometimes worked there, too. The friars felt it was their job to protect the women from attacks by soldiers or other men by keeping them locked in at night. The monjerío became dirty because so many people lived in the tiny rooms. Disease spread quickly because of the unclean living conditions.

There was much sickness throughout Mission San Gabriel Arcángel. The Spanish unknowingly brought germs with them. The neophytes had never been exposed to these germs, so their bodies were unable to fight them off. Diseases such as smallpox, **cholera**, and **dysentery** spread quickly among all in the missions and affected the mission's Native population.

LOSING PEOPLE FAST

In 1814, San Gabriel's friars wrote to the government, saying that the number of deaths at the mission was double the number of births. They reported that of the neophytes who were born, three out of four died before age two and very few reached adulthood. Frays José Mariá de Zalvidea and Gil y Taboada, leading the mission, pleaded in a report to the Spanish government to send doctors and medicine, or risk killing every Native person in California. That year Fray Zalvidea had a hospital built near the mission—it was always nearly full.

In 1825, an epidemic of smallpox and cholera spread through Mission San Gabriel Arcángel. It is estimated that three of every four neophytes died. Altogether, nearly 6,000 Native Americans are buried in the mission's cemetery, more than at any of California's other missions.

Many of the neophytes ran away, fearing sickness, punishment, and death. Some hid in the safety of the San Gabriel Mountains, which were unfamiliar to the Spanish. Others went to different regions and intermarried with other tribes. Disease claimed many others. The tribe was nearly gone.

8
Secularization

The Spanish government tried to respond to the complaints of the settlers who wanted the mission land. It passed laws to **secularize** California's missions, which means to make them nonreligious and take them from the control of Catholic friars. This was delayed because New Spain had begun a war of independence with Spain. In 1821, New Spain won its independence and became Mexico.

RELEASING THE LAND

In 1826, a law freed all neophytes who had been Christians for more than 15 years. Some neophytes gladly left the missions. Others did not want to leave the friars. Mission life was the only life they knew. On August 17, 1833, the Mexican government passed its final law secularizing the missions of upper and lower California. The missions would be called pueblos and fall under the supervision of government administrators. Mission San Gabriel Arcángel was secularized in 1834.

Much of the mission land was taken over by the settlers and the government, although it had been promised to the neophytes. A few neophytes were given mission land. However, many no longer wanted to herd and farm. They returned to their villages, only to find that settlers had taken the land. A large number of neophytes went to work at pueblos or ranchos. Most neophytes lost all they had.

POOR LEADERSHIP

An administrator, Colonel Nicolas Gutierrez, took over the new pueblo of San Gabriel. The mission's two friars, Frays Gonzalez de Ibarra and Tomás Estenga, fled in 1835. They were upset that the mission was falling apart under the careless leadership of Gutierrez and felt unable to help the neophytes who remained.

In 1842, the Mexican government panicked. The missions were not producing enough food or supplies for the presidios. San Gabriel and eleven other missions were returned to the friars. When Fray

The Mexican government and settlers wanted the land surrounding the Mission San Gabriel Arcángel.

Estenga returned to San Gabriel, almost everything was gone. Nearly all of the 16,500 cattle had been killed for their hides. Less than 100 remained. Most mission land was in the hands of strangers. The workshops and pantries were empty. The only neophytes left were the sick, the old, and some orphaned children.

In 1848, the United States won a war against Mexico and gained control of California, which two years later became the thirty-first state. President James Buchanan returned the mission property to the Catholic Church in 1859.

Today Mission San Gabriel Arcángel stands in the city of Los Angeles, offering visitors much to see and do.

9
The
Mission Today

Today, the mission sits in the middle of Los Angeles. Many visitors come to see its architecture, learn about its history in its museum, and admire its church.

BELLS CHIME AGAIN

An earthquake damaged the campanario in 1987. Another earthquake struck in 1994. After this, the U.S. federal government helped with its restoration. In 1996, on its 225th anniversary, Mission San Gabriel Arcángel's bells rang again.

The inside of the church still glows with the colors painted by the neophytes: deep red, gold, and forest green. The altar holds six carved wooden statues brought from Spain in 1791. The statue in the center is of Saint Gabriel. The original pulpit where the friars stood long ago and prayed with the neophytes remains intact.

On a wall hangs the 300-year-old painting of Our Lady of Sorrows, famous from the legend of the mission's founding. The museum displays the oldest-known paintings by neophytes, a series of paintings of the Stations of the Cross, which depict the events surrounding the crucifixion of Jesus.

DOOR TO THE PAST

While most of the mission buildings and workshops fell to ruins long ago, many of the foundations still remain. Visitors can see the restored winery, the friars' quarters, the original kitchen and the open fireplace, and the brick tanks of the tannery. There are also four brick-lined holes that were part of the soap and tallow factory. Carved into the bottom of one of the mission's wooden doors is a cat door. Because the mission had mice, one of the first things San Gabriel's friars requested from New Spain was a cat.

Visitors can also follow a path to the gardens. The corridor is shaded by three grape arbors with vines from the original vineyard. The first vine, planted in 1826, has grown so thick that it has cracked the cement around it. There are also replicas of all twenty-one missions built by students from Claretian Seminary (a school for training priests) in 1932. Outside the walls are the bricks from the 1775 bell tower.

Just outside the church is Mission San Gabriel Arcángel's cemetery. It is the oldest cemetery in Los Angeles County and the final resting place of thousands of men, women, and children who built the mission.

In 1908, the Claretian religious order, members of the Roman Catholic group the Missionary Sons of the Immaculate Heart of Mary, took over Mission San Gabriel Arcángel. They continue to operate San Gabriel Mission as a parish church in the Archdiocese of Los Angeles.

10
Make Your Own Mission Model

To make your own model of the San Gabriel Arcángel mission, you will need:

- construction paper (orange)
- Foam Core board
- glue
- miniature bells (6)
- paint (beige and green)
- pencil
- ruler
- Styrofoam
- toothpicks
- X-ACTO® knife

DIRECTIONS

Adult supervision is suggested.

Step 1: Cut out a piece of Foam Core measuring 20" × 20" (50.8 cm × 50.8 cm) for the mission base. Paint the base green. Allow it to dry.

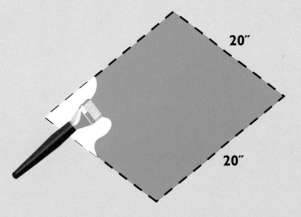

20"

20"

Step 2: Cut two pieces of Styrofoam that measure 9" × 9" (22.9 cm × 22.9 cm) to make the front and back of the church. Draw and then cut out a window and front door on one piece.

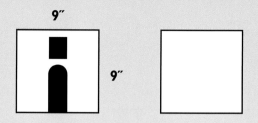

Step 3: Cut out a piece of Styrofoam that is 9" × 8" (22.9 cm × 20.3 cm). This will be the left side of the church. Paint all three walls beige.

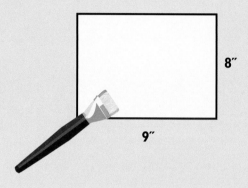

Step 4: Position the church walls on the base to form three sides of a box. Glue the pieces in place and let dry.

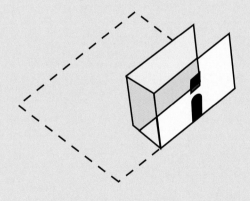

Step 5: Cut out three pieces of Styrofoam that are 20" × 4" (50.8 cm × 10.2 cm) and one piece that is 11" × 4" (27.9 cm × 10.2 cm).

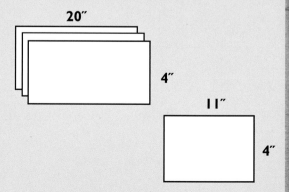

Step 6: Paint all four pieces beige. Allow them to dry. Glue them to the base around the edges so that they form the courtyard walls.

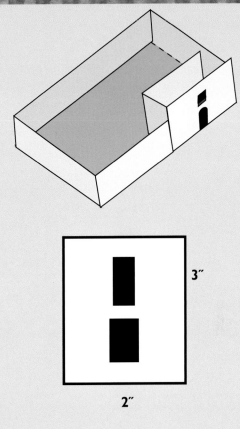

Step 7: Make a main bell tower by cutting a piece of Styrofoam that is 2″ × 3″ (5.1 cm × 7.6 cm). Draw and cut out two windows from the bell tower.

3″

2″

Step 8: Cut out a small half circle with a bottom measuring 2″ (5.1 cm). Cut out a window from it. Place this piece on top of the bell tower.

2″

Step 9: Place the bell tower on the board beside the church. Make two more small bell towers for the church by cutting six pieces of Styrofoam measuring 0.5″ × 1.5″ (1.3 cm × 3.8 cm).

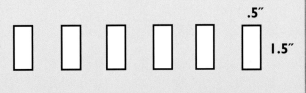

.5″

1.5″

Step 10: Glue a piece of Styrofoam measuring 0.5" × 1.5" (1.3 cm × 3.8 cm) on top of two other pieces measuring 0.5" × 1.5" (1.3 cm × 3.8 cm) as shown here. Repeat with the other three foam pieces and attach to the top of the church.

Step 11: Paint all Styrofoam pieces beige. Allow them to dry.

Step 12: Stick a toothpick through the top of a miniature bell and insert the end of the toothpick into the main bell tower. Do this with the other bells and insert into the other bell towers.

Step 13: Fold a piece of orange paper back and forth to make it appear rippled. Cut into strips and glue the ends of the paper to the front and back walls so that it stretches over the tops of the walls.

Step 14: Bend two strips of orange paper into a triangle and glue to the small towers. Cut out Styrofoam crosses and insert them in the top of the church with toothpicks.

Step 15: Decorate around the mission with greenery and flowers. You can make these decorations with colored tissue paper, or paint them directly onto the mission.

The model of Mission San Gabriel Arcángel when it is completed.

Key Dates in Mission History

1492	Christopher Columbus reaches the West Indies
1542	Cabrillo's expedition to California
1602	Sebastián Vizcaíno sails to California
1713	Fray Junípero Serra is born
1769	Founding of San Diego de Alcalá
1770	Founding of San Carlos Borroméo del Río Carmelo
1771	Founding of San Antonio de Padua and San Gabriel Arcángel
1772	Founding of San Luis Obispo de Tolosa
1775–76	Founding of San Juan Capistrano
1776	Founding of San Francisco de Asís
1776	Declaration of Independence is signed

1777	Founding of Santa Clara de Asís
1782	Founding of San Buenaventura
1784	Fray Serra dies
1786	Founding of Santa Bárbara
1787	Founding of La Purísima Concepción
1791	Founding of Santa Cruz and Nuestra Señora de la Soledad
1797	Founding of San José, San Juan Bautista, San Miguel Arcángel, and San Fernando Rey de España
1798	Founding of San Luis Rey de Francia
1804	Founding of Santa Inés
1817	Founding of San Rafael Arcángel
1823	Founding of San Francisco Solano
1833	Mexico passes Secularization Act
1848	Gold found in northern California
1850	California becomes the thirty-first state

Glossary

adobe (uh-DOH-bee) Brick made from dried mud and straw.

angelus (AN-jeh-les) A bell rung at morning, noon, and night to call Catholics to recite a prayer called the Angelus.

baptism (BAP-tih-zum) Welcoming a person to Christianity by a ceremony that involves covering or sprinkling him or her with water.

Catholicism (kuh-THAH-luh-sih-zum) The religion of the Catholic Church.

cholera (KAH-luh-ruh) An infectious disease that causes problems in the intestines.

dysentery (DIH-sen-ter-ee) A disease of the large intestine.

Franciscan (fran-SIS-ken) A member of a Roman Catholic group founded by Saint Francis of Assisi in Italy in 1209.

Moors (MOORZ) A group of North African Arab people who ruled parts of Spain from the eighth century until 1492.

secularize (SEH-kyoo-luh-ryz) To take control away from the church and its priests and give it to the government and citizens.

shaman (SHAH-man) A Native American religious leader and healer.

viceroy (VYS-roy) A governor who rules and acts as the representative of the king.

Pronunciation Guide

alcaldes (ol-KOL-des)

campanario (kam-pah-NAH-ree-oh)

convento (kom-BEN-toh)

El Camino Real (EL kah-MEE-noh RAY-al)

mayordomo (mah-yor-DOH-moh)

temblores (tem-BLOR-ays)

wots (WOTS)

Find Out More

To learn more about the California missions, check out these books, websites, and videos:

BOOKS

Bibby, Brian. *The Fine Art of California Indian Basketry.* Berkeley, CA: Heydey, 2013.

Duffield, Katy S. *California History for Kids.* Chicago, IL: Chicago Review Press, 2012.

Gendell, Megan. *The Spanish Missions of California.* New York, NY: Scholastic, 2010.

Weber, Matt. *California's Missions A to Z.* San Francisco, CA: 121 Publications, 2010.

WEBSITES

California Missions Board Game

edweb.sdsu.edu/courses/edtec670/Cardboard/Board/C/Calmission/index.html

Playing this game will reinforce concepts and ideas learned about the twenty-one missions. Designed for the classroom, the goal of this game is to be the first traveling friar to travel from the most southern mission (Mission San Diego de Alcalá) to the most northern mission (Mission San Francisco Solano). Friars must deal with various setbacks and obstacles as they choose from various paths along the game board.

California Missions Resource Center

www.missionscalifornia.com/missions

Learn more about mission leaders, view photographs and architectural drawings of the mission property. Check out the "Ask The Experts" page to view frequently asked questions about the missions, or search the website and submit your own.

Keepers of Indigenous Ways

www.keepersofindigenousways.org

Explore the villages of the Tongva people. Learn more about their culture, language, arts, and sacred sites.

VIDEO

California Missions DVDs

www.calgold.com/missions

(855) 994-8355

Follow Huell Howser and cameraman Luis Fuerte as they set out on a quest to explore all twenty-one missions that run much of the length of present-day California. The miniseries features three missions in each thirty-minute episode. Get a better understanding of just what it is about these missions that continues to captivate so many people after all these years. Individual mission DVDs also available.

Index

Page numbers in **boldface** are illustrations.